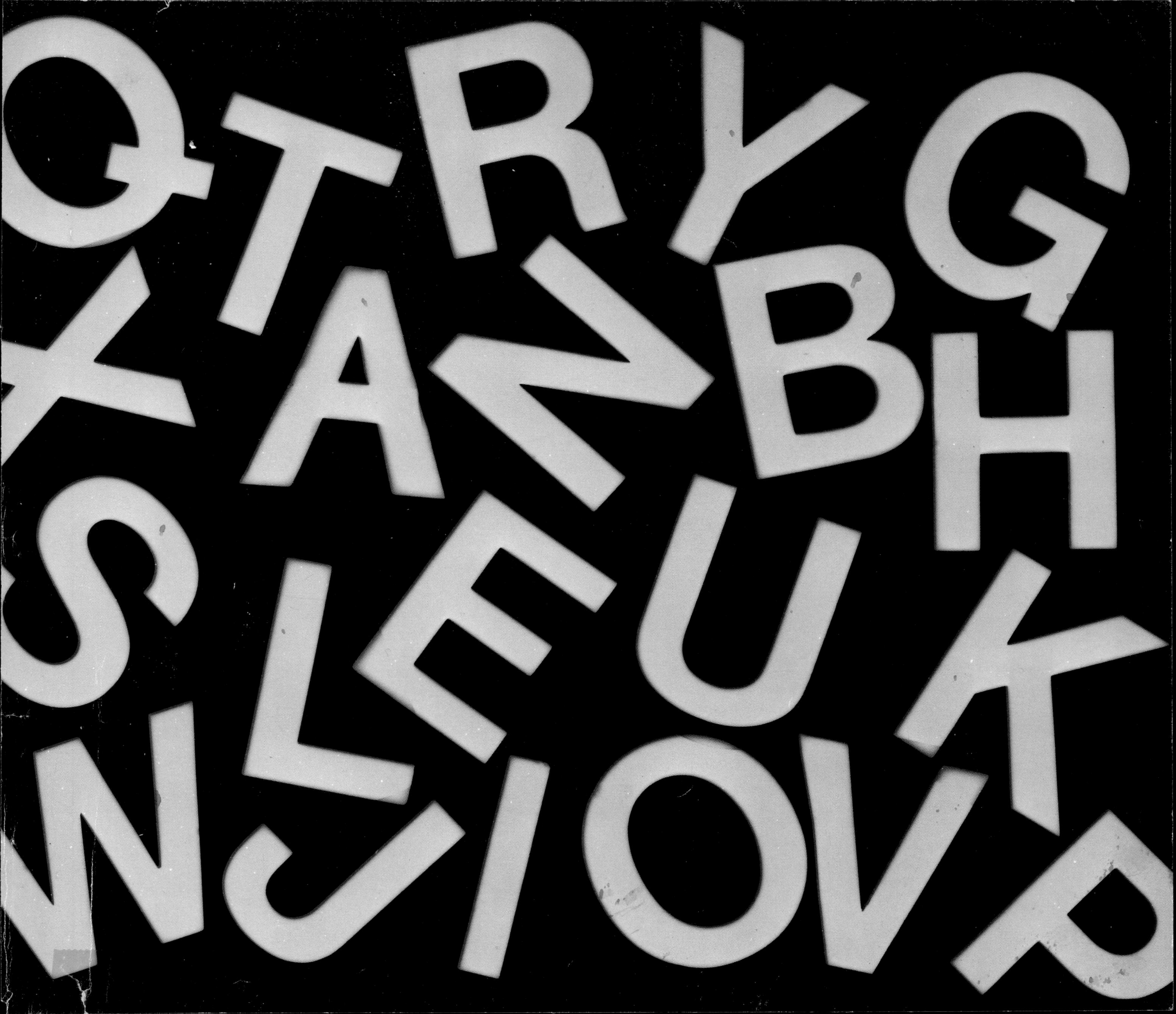

A, B, See!

by TANA HOBAN

Greenwillow Books, New York

ibrary of Congress
ataloging in Publication Data
oban, Tana.
, B, see!
ummary: A collection of photograms
f objects which begin with a
articular letter of the alphabet.
, English language—Alphabet—Juvenile
terature. [1. Alphabet] I. Title.
E1155.H58   [E]   81-6890
BN 0-688-00832-1   AACR2
BN 0-688-00833-X (lib. bdg.)

This one is
for Miela

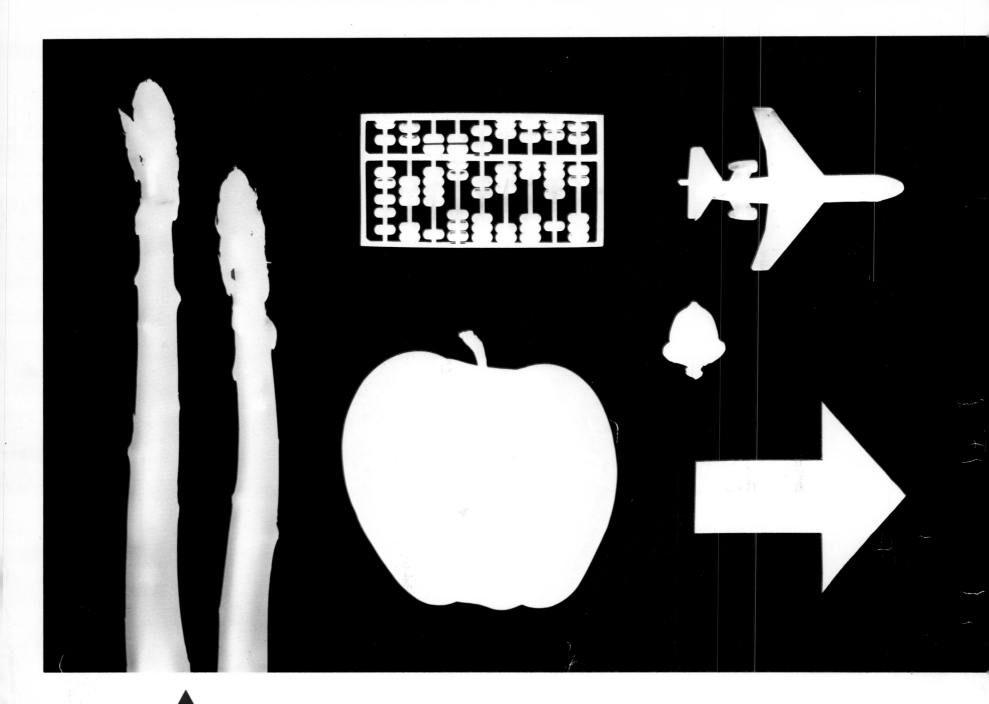

A BCDEFGHIJKLMNOPQRSTUVWXYZ

aBCDEFGHIJKLMNOPQRSTUVWXYZ

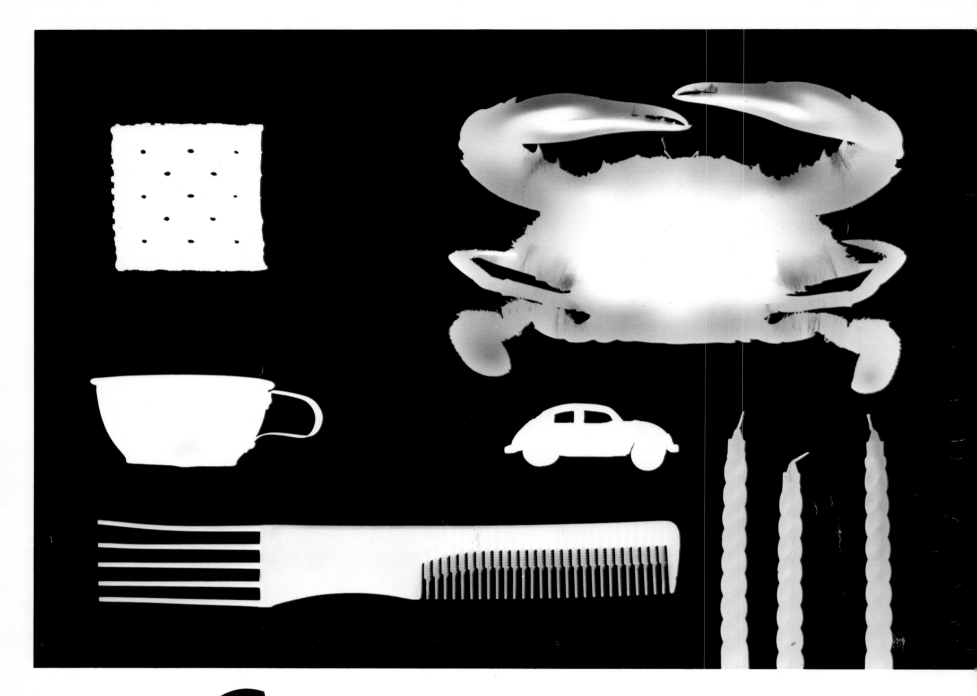

ABCDEFGHIJKLMNOPQRSTUVWXYZ

D

ABCDEFGHIJKLMNOPQRSTUVWXYZ

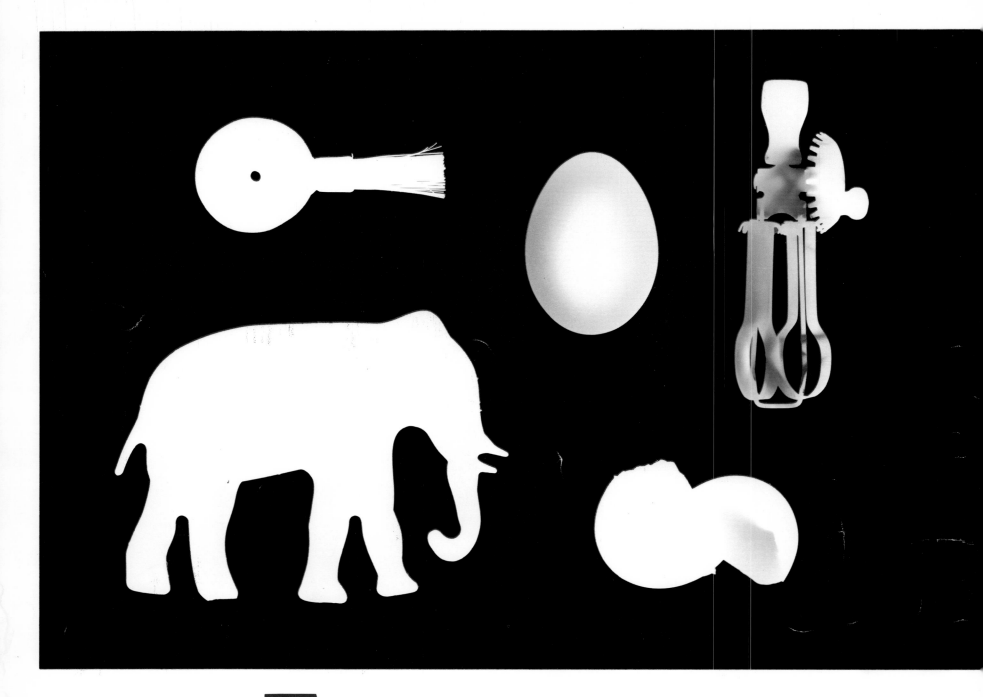

ABCD**E**FGHIJKLMNOPQRSTUVWXYZ

ABCDE **F** GHIJKLMNOPQRSTUVWXYZ

ABCDEF**G**HIJKLMNOPQRSTUVWXYZ

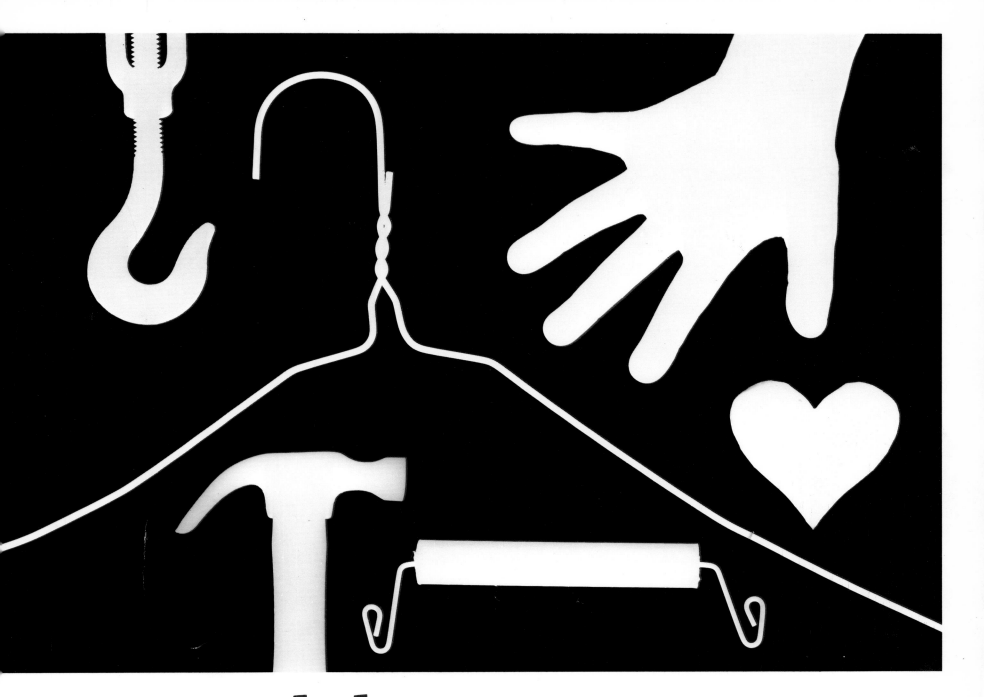

ABCDEFG**H**IJKLMNOPQRSTUVWXYZ

ABCDEFGH I JKLMNOPQRSTUVWXYZ

ABCDEFGHI J KLMNOPQRSTUVWXYZ

K

ABCDEFGHIJ**K**LMNOPQRSTUVWXYZ

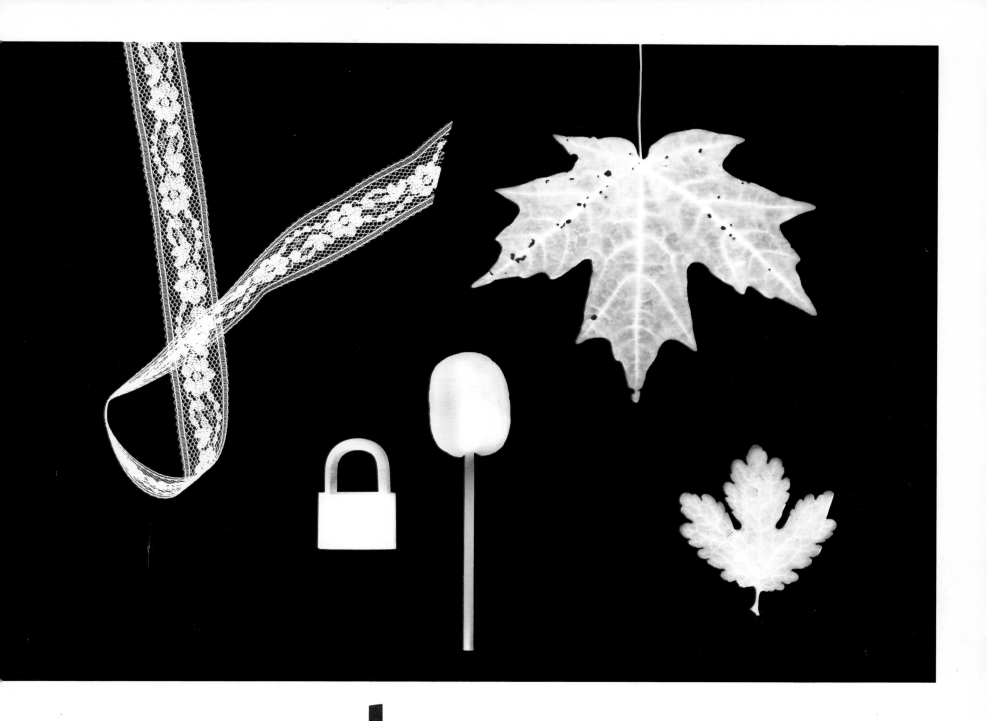

L

ABCDEFGHIJK**L**MNOPQRSTUVWXYZ

ABCDEFGHIJKL**M**NOPQRSTUVWXYZ

9

N

ABCDEFGHIJKLMNOPQRSTUVWXYZ

ABCDEFGHIJKLMN**O**PQRSTUVWXYZ

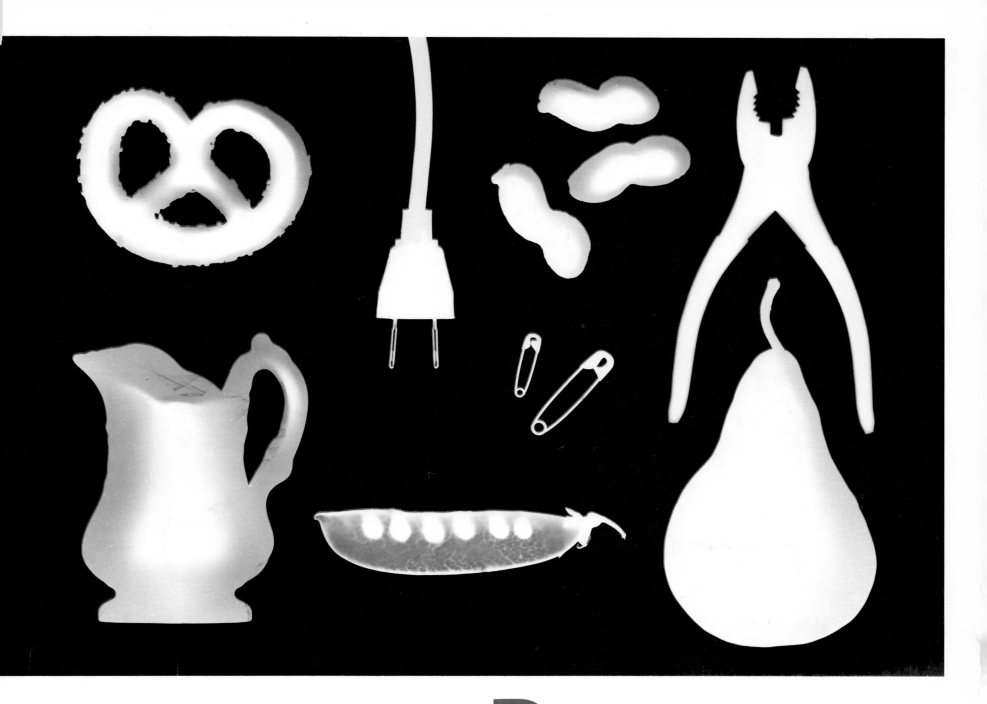

ABCDEFGHIJKLMNO**P**QRSTUVWXYZ

ABCDEFGHIJKLMNOP**Q**RSTUVWXYZ

R

ABCDEFGHIJKLMNOPQ**R**STUVWXYZ

ABCDEFGHIJKLMNOPQR**S**TUVWXYZ

T

ABCDEFGHIJKLMNOPQRSTUVWXYZ

ABCDEFGHIJKLMNOPQRST**U**VWXYZ

ABCDEFGHIJKLMNOPQRSTU**V**WXYZ

ABCDEFGHIJKLMNOPQRSTUV**W**XYZ

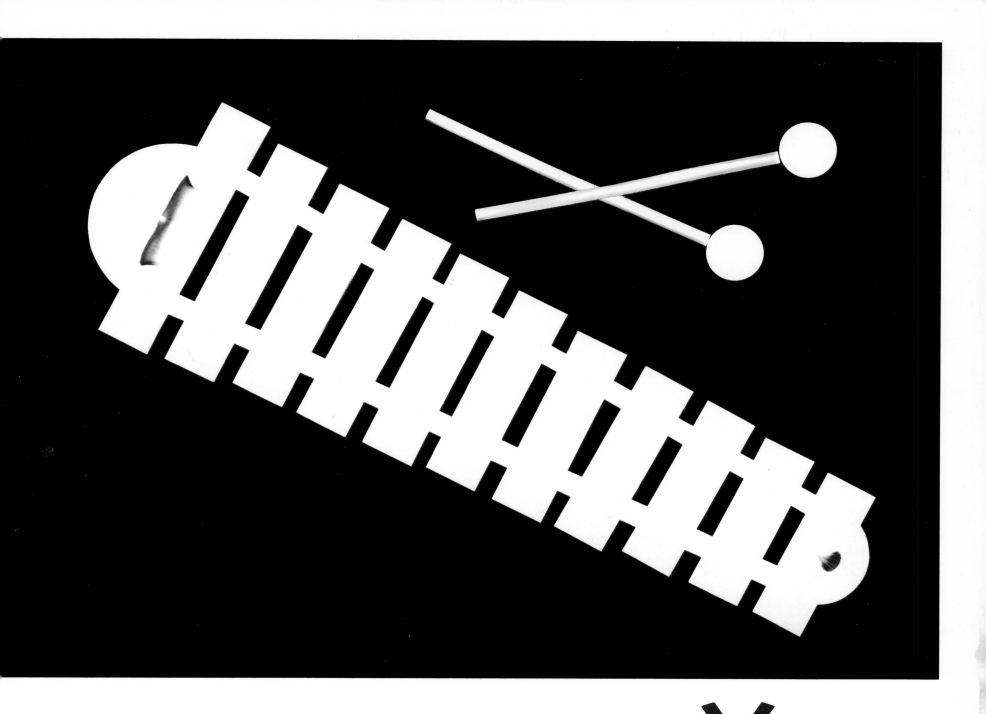

ABCDEFGHIJKLMNOPQRSTUVW**X**yz

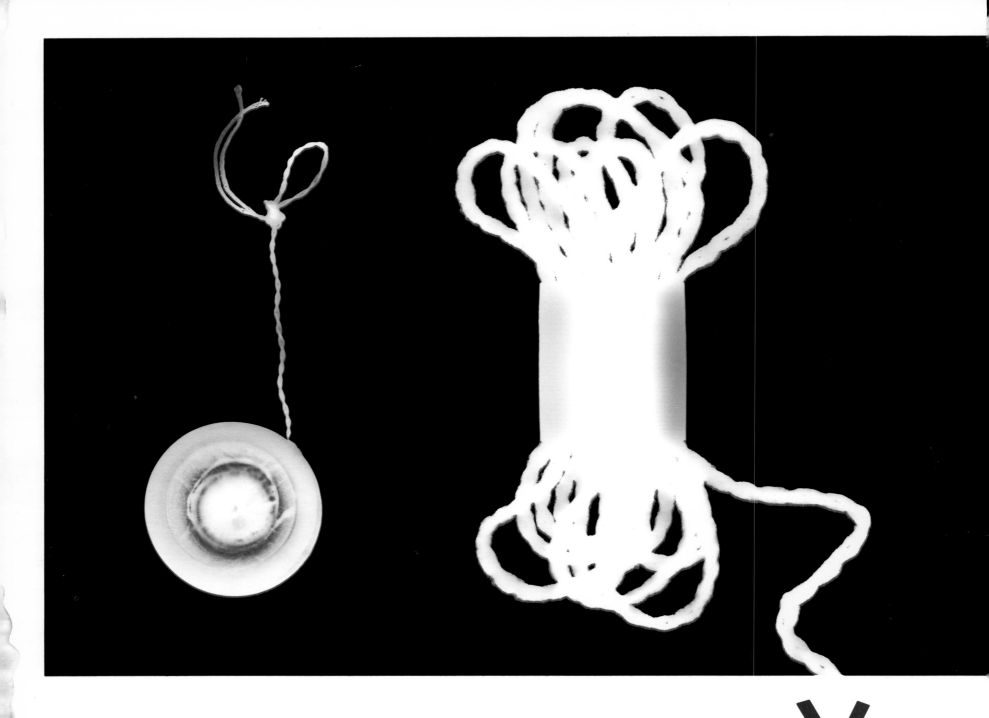

ABCDEFGHIJKLMNOPQRSTUVWXYz

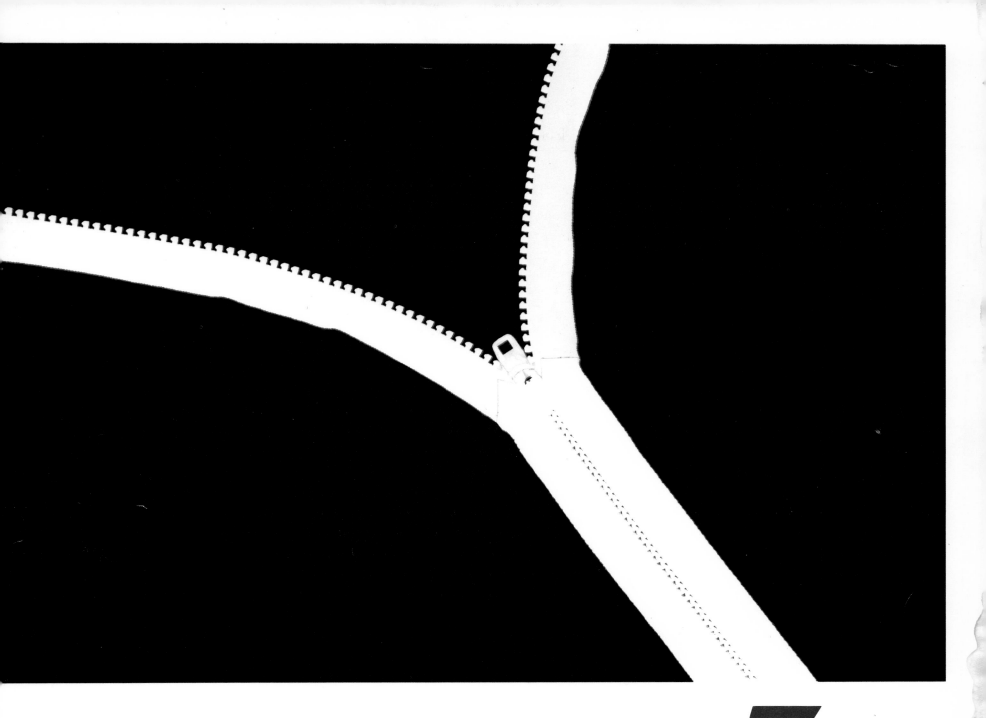

ABCDEFGHIJKLMNOPQRSTUVWXYZ

TANA HOBAN's photographs
have been exhibited at the
Museum of Modern Art. She has
won many gold medals and prizes
for her work as a photographer and
filmmaker. And, of course, her
books for children are known and
loved throughout the world.